WHAT EVERY WOMAN NEEDS TO KNOW ABOUT SEXUAL ASSAULT

Editorial Assistance Provided by
Citizens Against Crime, Inc.

GUARDIAN PRESS

Copyright 1993, Guardian Press
All Rights Reserved

ISBN 0-9632355-2-4

No part of this book may be used or reproduced in any manner whatsoever without written permission of the publisher, except in the case of brief quotations embodied in critical articles or reviews.

Crime prevention techniques cited in this book were obtained from various outside sources, including, but not limited to, federal, state and local law enforcement officials and crime prevention experts. We believe the information to be accurate and reliable. However, we do not warrant the accuracy or reliability of the information contained herein.

Furthermore, Guardian Press makes no guarantees of results from the use of information contained herein. We assume no liability in connection with either the information contained in this book or the crime prevention suggestions made. Moreover, we would caution that it cannot be assumed that every acceptable crime prevention procedure is contained in this book. Obviously, abnormal, unusual or individual circumstances may require further or additional procedures.

To order additional copies of this book, call
Citizens Against Crime, Inc.

1-800-466-1010

ACKNOWLEDGMENTS

Guardian Press would like to thank the following organizations and individuals whose cooperation and suggestions helped make this book possible.

In alphabetical order:

* Citizens Against Crime, Inc.

* Federal Bureau of Investigation, U.S. Department of Justice

* Houston Police Department, Crime Prevention Unit

* Dr. Gail Hudson, University of Houston

* Janice E. Rench, L.S.W.

Editors: Allison Victoria Eaves and Betty L. Eaves
Cover Design: Aloana Keaton
Page Layout and Design: Arthur S. Lobato
Research Assistant: Beth Eaves

CONTENTS

The Grim Statistics — 1

Introduction — 3

What is Sexual Assault? — 5

The Frequency of Sexual Assault — 7

The Myths of Sexual Assault — 9

Who is the Rapist? — 13

What Motivates the Rapist? — 15

Who is the Most Likely Victim? — 19

Where does Sexual Assault Occur? — 20

Precautionary Measures — 21

Precautions to Take in Your Home or Apartment — 22

Precautions to Take in and around Your Car — 29

Precautions to Take on the Street — 36

Precautions to Take while Traveling 41

Precautions to Take with Dates and Acquaintances 43

Danger Signs to Watch for in a Date or Acquaintance 47

Protect Yourself at All Times 50

Individual Reactions to Sexual Assault 53

Tactics to Use if Attacked 55

What to Do if You Are Sexually Assaulted 63

How Family and Friends Can Help the Victim of a Sexual Assault 68

FOREWORD

The subject of violence against women has received considerable attention over the last decade. Professionals from many disciplines and for a wide variety of purposes have focused on the causes, the offenders, the victims, treatment and prevention. We continue to learn and have a better understanding about the complexities of this crime. Partially due to this increased knowledge, victims have had the courage to come forward and report the crime. Whether the increase in statistics reflects an increase in actual violence being committed against women or just a better method of collecting data is not yet clear. But there are two things that are very clear: this violence is widespread, and it fundamentally alters the way women view the world around them.

First, violence against women has been reported in every corner of our country. It cuts across every age, race, religious and economic segment of our community. Secondly, what is often overlooked when people read statistics is the effect the threat of actual violence has on women. The mere possibility of sexual violence alters one's interpretation of the world. Surely, any attempt to comprehend the lives of women, without taking into account the issues of violence against them, is misguided. Every female from an early age is conditioned to alter her life, thoughts and movements in order to compensate for verbal, emotional or physical assaults against her. In order to fight against this most prevalent crime, women need to have accurate information and be empowered to protect themselves.

WHAT EVERY WOMAN NEEDS TO KNOW ABOUT SEXUAL ASSAULT provides both these things to anyone who reads this book. Written in a straightforward and concise manner, it contains accurate information and gives practical and useful suggestions for lowering one's risk for being the next victim. I highly recommend that this book be in every home, every junior and senior high school, and every college and university.

Janice E. Rench, L.S.W.

Author, Counselor and
National Lecturer on
Victimization against
Women and Children

THE GRIM STATISTICS

1. Since the mid-1970s, sexual assault has become the fastest growing violent crime in America. Between 1990 and 1991, the U.S. Department of Justice reported a 59% increase in reported rapes and attempted rapes in the U.S.

2. At the present time, one woman in four will be a victim of sexual assault in her lifetime. If rapes continue to increase at the 1990 - 1991 levels, it will soon be one woman out of three and then one out of two.

3. More than 60% of rapes are committed by a person known to the victim. On college campuses, 84% of the victims knew their attacker.

4. In 14% of reported rapes, the attacker is a close friend, a member of the family or a close family friend.

5. In more than 80% of reported rapes, the victim and the attacker are of the same race and socio-economic background.

6. Most rapes occur in the home of the victim or the home of the attacker.

7. Only 5% of rape victims report their attack to the police. Fewer than 45% of rape victims tell anyone about their attack.

8. Almost 90% of rapes involve threats of physical harm or the actual use of physical force.

9. The youngest reported rape victim was two months old. The oldest victim was 92.

10. Nearly 80% of convicted rapists who are released from prison will commit seven more rapes before being arrested again.

INTRODUCTION

Sexual assault is a violent act of aggression committed against females of all ages. While it is a crime that is also committed against males, particularly young boys, women are its victims more than 95% of the time.

Since the mid-1970s, the number of reported rapes in the United States has increased faster than any other violent crime. And only a fraction of all rapes are actually reported! Most rapes involve some sort of physical force or threat of force with a weapon.

There is no pattern to the crime. Sexual assault occurs in the home and in the workplace, at the mall and the corner store, in kindergartens and on college campuses, it happens in the morning, afternoon and evening, to the plain and the beautiful, to the young and the old. It is a crime that degrades its victims and violates the most basic rights of freedom. It can happen to any woman or child, any time, any place. A vulnerable target and the right opportunity are the only two elements a rapist needs. Almost without exception, it happens when it's least expected. The element of surprise always works in the rapist's favor.

The intent of this book is not to frighten you, but to enlighten you about the realities of sexual assault and the terrible impact it has on its victims. It is our hope that the following information will help keep it from ever happening to you or your loved ones.

WHAT IS SEXUAL ASSAULT?

Sexual assault, or rape, occurs when a victim is deprived of freedom of choice and is forced or coerced to commit sexual acts under duress. Rape almost always is committed by a male upon an unconsenting female.

Although the legal definition of rape varies from state to state, most laws define rape as "sexual contact that occurs under actual or threatened force and against the will of the victim." Any time a woman is forced to have sex without consent, she has been sexually assaulted.

A victim can be sexually assaulted in a number of circumstances.

1. Date or Acquaintance Rape

This happens when a woman is forced or coerced to have sex by someone she knows, such as a date or acquaintance. Females in junior and senior high school and college are particularly vulnerable to date rape. *More than half of all rapes are committed by a date or acquaintance of the victim.* A high incidence of date rape occurs during spring break.

2. Stranger Rape

This occurs when when a person is raped by a total stranger. The assailant, acting alone, often uses sexual assault to vent his rage, frustration or feelings of impotence.

3. Gang Rape

This takes place when a person is raped by two or more assailants. Men who band together in groups or teams are more likely to be involved in this crime. Street gangs, groups of servicemen, members of fraternities and members of sports teams frequently are the assailants in gang rapes.

4. Statutory Rape

This occurs when an adult has sexual intercourse with a person under the age of consent, even if the victim is willing. Eighteen is the age of consent in most states, but it varies from state to state.

THE FREQUENCY OF SEXUAL ASSAULT

Nationwide crime reports indicate that a rape occurs every five minutes in America. These statistics are based solely on reported rapes. The incidence of sexual assault may actually be much greater due to the fact that many rape victims are reluctant to report the crime. Only 5% of rape victims report the crime to the police. For that reason, no accurate figures exist on the frequency of the crime. However, by some estimates, two million rapes take place in the United States each year--one about every 15 seconds.

Various surveys conducted in recent years indicate that an alarming number of women have been victims of some sort of sexual coercion or forced sexual activities. Several such surveys, conducted at colleges and in the military, revealed that between 50% and 60% of the women who participated in the study had either been the victim or near-victim of sexual assault.

As these surveys and crime reports seem to indicate, women and children are at great risk of becoming victims of this horrible crime. Why is sexual assault so prevalent in our society? What causes men to rape women? Is it for sexual gratification, or does it involve much deeper psychological and social issues? Part of the answer is based on fact. Much of what we perceive, however, is based on myth.

THE MYTHS OF SEXUAL ASSAULT

There are many misconceptions about sexual assault that continue to prevail without basis in fact. Some concern the victim, others the assailant.

The Myth: "Rape victims are always young and attractive."

Unfortunately, movie and television dramatizations continue to perpetuate this fallacy. The truth is, there is no such person as the "typical victim." Cases of sexual assault have been reported involving victims as young as two months of age and as old as 92. In reality, physical appearance has little to do with rape in most cases. Vulnerability, not physical appearance, is a major factor in sexual assault.

The Myth: "The woman provokes the attack."

This is a tired old myth that attempts to place the blame for the attack on the actions or mode of dress of the victim. Sadly, this is often dredged up as a defense for the assailant. The fact is, the assailant chooses his victim on the basis of opportunity and then initiates the attack. The rapist almost always selects a victim who appears vulnerable and alone.

The Myth: "Most rapists are black and their victims are white."

This myth is steeped in racial prejudice and is totally false. In actuality, white men rape black women twice as often as black men rape white women. But a far more important statistic reveals that the victim and the rapist are of the same race and socio-economic background in more than 80% of rape cases.

The Myth: "It's physically impossible to have sex with a woman against her will."

The idea that any woman can successfully resist rape "if she really wants to" is totally false. Even a woman who fights back with all her might can be overpowered if the attacker is physically stronger. In many cases of date rape, women submit to their attacker purely out of fear of physical harm or death. Almost 90% of rapes involve either threats of physical harm or actual physical force against the victim. Oftentimes, too, the attacker threatens the victim with a weapon, greatly increasing the chance of physical injury or death from resisting. Sometimes, as in gang rape, there is more than one assailant. It would be difficult enough to fight off one attacker, let alone two or more. Finally, the rapist has the element of surprise on his side. A woman who is caught off guard--as many are--and attacked by surprise is far less able to ward off her attacker.

The Myth: "It can't happen to me."

Many women have deluded themselves into thinking that they could never be the victim of sexual assault. This may be because of their age, their physical appearance, their life-style or their occupation. The truth is, every female is a potential victim of sexual assault. By some estimates, one woman out of four will be raped during her lifetime. It would appear that many women have been victimized to some degree by this crime. Just the threat of sexual assault has made it far more difficult for women to lead independent lives. Many have had to change their routines, life-styles, occupations or places of residence out of fear of being attacked.

The Myth: "Men rape for sexual gratification."

This, too, is just a myth. Numerous studies dealing with rapists indicate that they often have consenting sexual relationships, either with a spouse or companion, yet they still choose to rape for one reason or another. Some rape because they enjoy overpowering and degrading their victims; others may use rape to vent their feelings of hostility, aggression or inferiority. Sex is not the motivating factor, only the chosen mode of expression. In reality, the crime of rape bears no resemblance at all to normal sexual activities. Rape more closely resembles violent crimes like robbery and aggravated assault than it does sexual intercourse between consenting adults.

The Myth: "The rapist is usually a stranger to the victim."

Nothing could be further from the truth. Most women are raped by someone they know. Within the general population, the rapist is a date, acquaintance or relative more than 60% of the time. On college campuses, 84% of rape victims knew their attacker.

The Myth: "Women often lie about being raped to protect their reputation."

This is another myth that attempts to discredit the victim. However, the facts don't lie. Only about 2% of rape reports turn out to be false, which happens to be the same as false reports for other felonies. If anything, women tend not to report rapes. By some estimates, less than 5% of rapes are actually reported to the police or to rape crisis centers.

WHO IS THE RAPIST ?

There is no stereotypical profile of a rapist. Rapists come from all walks of life, from all ethnic groups, from all social and economic levels. The rapist often appears to be a normal individual, but in reality, he is very likely a person who has difficulty relating to others in a permanent or lasting fashion. He also may fear or resent women. Although he may be emotionally unstable, the rapist is able to deal with life on a day-to-day basis in a reasonably normal and competent manner. More than 66% of convicted rapists were either married or had a relationship with a consenting sex partner.

Some sex offenders have been found to be heavy viewers of sexually violent pornography that subjugates or denigrates women. Still others used sexually explicit materials during adolescence and adulthood. These men sometimes tend to view women more as objects to be used than as human beings. Also, men with exhibitionistic or voyeuristic tendencies may be potentially dangerous if their abnormal behavior is only one part of a fantasy which also includes rape.

Sexual assault often is committed by persons under the influence of drugs or alcohol. Some men who otherwise appear to be law-abiding citizens can turn ugly and violent when they are using drugs or alcohol. About 75% of men involved in date or acquaintance rape had been drinking or taking drugs before the attack. However, being intoxicated or under the influence of drugs is no excuse for rape.

In some cases, the rapist and the victim are complete strangers. In the majority of cases, however, the rapist is a friend, a date, a relative, a co-worker or a casual acquaintance. In short, it is difficult if not impossible to know if a particular man has the potential to be a rapist. This is not stated as an indictment of males in general, nor is it meant to suggest that you view all men with suspicion. Most men are loving, caring individuals who find rape to be a heinous crime. We do, however, suggest a certain degree of wariness and caution when you are in the company of men. The fact is, males commit the vast majority of rapes. Even men who look and act normal are capable of this violent act.

In many cases of gang rape, a mob mentality prevails. Men who otherwise would not rape in a one-on-one situation might participate in a gang rape. These individuals usually are easily controlled by a leader who may instigate the attack. Men who participate in gang rape may be seeking the validation and approval of other males in the group.

WHAT MOTIVATES THE RAPIST?

Actually, there is no single motive for the violent crime of rape. Instead, there appears to be a range of causes, depending on the emotional state of the rapist and the circumstances of the rape. Feelings of extreme anger, sadistic feelings and the need for power appear to motivate many rapists. While the need for sexual release sometimes is given as a reason for rape, most authorities discount this as a motivation. All men need sexual release. However, they all do not commit rape to get that release.

It cannot be emphasized too strongly that sexual assault is a crime of extreme violence and aggression. Rapists almost always view their victims as objects to be exploited sexually to vent their hostility, aggression, frustration or insecurity. They obviously do not see their victim as a fellow human being at the moment of attack. All too often, the intent of rapists is to humiliate and degrade their victims. In many cases, the fantasy which rapists are acting out carries with it the danger of battery, assault with a deadly weapon or torture, in addition to the act of rape itself.

Although the following are not the only

motivations for sexual assault, they are the reasons most commonly cited by rape counselors and crime prevention experts.

1. Power and Control

Power rape is motivated mainly by the assailant's need to exert control over another human being. This type of rapist often is a person who feels powerless, vulnerable and insecure and possibly is overwhelmed by a sense of failure. Rape may be a way for him to gain the power that is missing in his life. His intent usually is to achieve control over his victim, not necessarily to physically injure her. He normally will use only enough force to cause his victim to cooperate submissively.

In some cases, the rapist may select a victim in advance and plan his assault. He sometimes is a serial rapist, committing his crime over and over again with the attacks increasing in frequency with time. Many young men on college campuses qualify as serial rapists, since they rape repeatedly.

There also is the danger of planned rapes at parties. Such parties usually involve consumption of large volumes of alcohol in order to make the women "more agreeable" or less able to resist unwanted sexual contact. All too often, the "party" is a game of power and control that manifests itself in rape. Also, it is not uncommon at such parties for women to be sexually assaulted after they become so intoxicated that they pass out. A rapist has the ultimate control over a victim who is unconscious.

Rapes involving power and control also occur frequently on dates. The rapist may erroneously perceive that the victim has done something to obligate herself to him. For example, a man may take a woman on a date and spend money on her. He then may wrongfully assume that the woman is obligated to perform sexually to "pay him back." If he isn't deterred by the woman's refusal and he forces or coerces her into having sex with him, the man is committing rape. *Any time a woman is made to commit sexual acts against her will, she has been raped, regardless of the circumstances.*

Men who commit power rape may be acting out some of the themes in our culture that glorify Hollywood's version of the strong, virile male who always gets what he wants--even if he has to take it by force. In reality, these men need to gain power because they feel powerless and are not truly secure about their manhood.

2. Anger

When anger and resentment are manifested in sexual assault, the attack can be savage and unpremeditated. It is often characterized by the use of physical violence that goes well beyond what is needed to force the victim to submit. This type of rapist often feels a deep sense of hostility toward women and uses rape as a way to "get even." The victim is often beaten or subjected to extreme degradation.

The unfortunate victim is usually a total stranger who just happens to be in the wrong place at the wrong time. This type of rape almost always is impulsive rather than planned and usually is triggered by something that pushes the rapist beyond the breaking point (marital conflict, loss of a job, financial difficulties, pressures at school, etc.).

3. Sadism

Rapes involving sadism often are preplanned rituals involving bondage, torture and sexual degradation. Aggression usually is an erotic experience for the sadistic rapist. He also may repeat the crime over and over.

This type of rapist may either target and stalk a victim beforehand, or he may cruise neighborhood streets or night clubs looking for a vulnerable person to be his victim. In some cases, gang rape is part of a sadistic ritual.

WHO IS THE MOST LIKELY VICTIM ?

Every female is a potential victim of sexual assault. *Every* female, regardless of race or age, regardless of social or economic status, regardless of life-style or locale.

The most vulnerable target is the woman who is alone at any time of day or night. She may be in her home, in her car, out shopping or on a date; she may be baby-sitting, walking through a parking garage, waiting at a bus stop or out jogging. When a woman is alone, she is always a potential rape victim.

While a relatively large number of reported victims fall into the 13-25 year old age bracket, indications are that this is due to an increased reporting rate in this age group. It also may be due to the increasing incidence of sexual assault on college campuses. Studies do not indicate any age preference by rapists, nor do they support the myth that sexual assault is provoked by either a woman's mode of dress or her mannerisms.

Vulnerability and opportunity are the key factors, regardless of everything else, that cause females of all ages to become victims of sexual assault.

WHERE DOES SEXUAL ASSAULT OCCUR?

Rape can and does occur virtually anywhere, but the largest single grouping of reported incidents is either in the home of the victim or in the home of the assailant. However, it is important to be aware of all potentially dangerous areas:

* Homes and apartments
* College dormitories (especially co-ed dorms)
* School campuses
* Hotel rooms
* Public restrooms
* Remote areas and vacant lots
* Public parks
* Dark or deserted streets
* Alleys
* Deserted buildings
* Building stairwells and elevators
* Parking lots and garages
* Beaches at night
* School playgrounds
* Shopping centers and malls
* Laundromats
* Self-service car washes

PRECAUTIONARY MEASURES

There is no doubt that the threat of sexual assault has greatly disrupted the lives of women. As stated earlier, many women have become victims of this crime to some degree because many have had to radically alter their lives to reduce their chances of being raped. If you heed the suggestions that follow, you too will have to make some adjustments in your life.

Some of the precautions may seem rather basic. Others may sound extreme. However, they are all necessary for your safety. The most difficult target for a rapist is a woman who is constantly on the alert, aware of her vulnerability at all times--in the home, in the car, on the street, while traveling or while out on a date. Your best protection against rape is a good defense. And there is no better defense than the right mix of concentration, caution and awareness.

PRECAUTIONS TO TAKE IN YOUR HOME OR APARTMENT

1. All exterior doors should be metal or have a solid wood core, as should the door from your garage to your house. Hollow-core doors offer very little resistance to the determined rapist or burglar.

2. Use good quality deadbolt locks on all exterior doors, including the door from the garage to the house. Make sure the deadbolt extends at least 1 1/2" into the door frame. Install a metal strike plate as well. This will make it more difficult for an attacker to kick in your door. (Most experts recommend either a deadbolt lock that requires a key or a pin tumbler cylinder lock. We suggest that you check with a locksmith for the best recommendation.)

3. Brace exterior doors from the inside as extra protection against an attacker kicking in your door. Wedge a chair under the door knob. There are even rods and other devices you can purchase that either are wedged under the door knob or the bottom of the door. Make sure the device you choose can be removed easily when you need to go out the door.

4. Have the locks on all exterior doors re-keyed when you move into a new house or apartment--or if you ever lose your keys. Have all work done by a licensed locksmith unless you are adept at do-it-yourself projects.

5. Install a peephole viewer with a minimum 180-degree angle in the front door. A peephole is inexpensive and easy to install. Use it to check out who is at the door every time. *Never* automatically open the door to a stranger. And don't rely on a chain lock. It is *not* a security device.

6. The locks on sliding glass doors are usually inadequate. However, you can secure them with inexpensive key locks or by a hole drilled through the overlapping frames and pinned with a nail. You can also use anti-slide blocks. And you can have screws protruding in the track to prevent the door from being lifted out.

7. Install extra window locks. The ordinary sash fastener offers virtually no resistance to an accomplished burglar or rapist. Sliding glass windows can be secured in the same fashion as sliding glass doors. Double-hung windows need either a sash fastener that can be locked with a key or a key lock built into the bottom window bar. You can also use eyebolts to lock windows to the frame. Remove operator handles from awning windows, but keep them nearby in case of fire.

8. Install storm windows. They provide an extra deterrent in that they force an intruder to break two panes of glass to get inside.

9. Install a locking device on your garage door. Drill a hole in the track that holds the door and insert either a pin or a padlock to prevent the door from being raised. Always keep your garage door closed and locked except when you're moving your car in and out.

10. Replace all jalousie doors and windows if possible. However, if this is not feasible, you can secure them by using a heavy gauge mesh or grillwork, but be sure they have a quick release feature on the inside for use in case of fire.

11. Install an alarm system, and place decals on your windows and a sign out front to warn intruders of its presence. But don't let the alarm system lull you into a false sense of security. You still need to maintain your vigil and take other steps to prevent a break-in. (If you can't afford an alarm system, purchase "dummy" decals and signs to make it appear that you have a system.)

12. Get in the habit of using all the security systems you install. Some 40% of intruders get into homes using virtually no force at all.

13. Good lighting can be a deterrent to a potential burglar or rapist. Install adequate exterior lighting at all entrances to the house. In an apartment, join with other tenants in demanding good lighting around the entrances and in hallways, parking areas, courtyards and laundry and game rooms.

14. Never open the door to strangers. Check the identity of callers through the peephole in the door, and instruct your children to get you if the caller is someone they don't know. In fact, it's a good idea not to let your children answer the door at all.

15. If someone comes to the door asking to use the phone for an emergency, offer to make the call for the person, but don't let the stranger inside your house.

16. Request identification of all repairmen and maintenance men who come to your door. Check their credentials by calling the company. However, use the number in the phone book, not the one on the I.D. card. In an apartment, call the apartment manager. Be especially leery of service or maintenance people who show up at your door without your having requested their services.

17. Be alert to suspicious phone calls. Do not give out personal or family information or information about your neighbors regardless of who the caller says he represents. Instruct your children to do the same.

18. Don't advertise that you live alone. When answering the door call out a "fake" name like, "I'll get it, Tom." List only your last name and first initials on the mailbox and in the telephone book. Consider adding "dummy" names on your mailbox to give the appearance of having roommates.

19. While at home at night, keep a light on in more than one room to make it appear that you're not alone. While away from your dwelling at night, make it look and sound occupied. Leave a radio on, and turn on lights in more than one room plus the bathroom.

20. If you live in an apartment, avoid going to the laundry room alone, especially at night. And don't take out the garbage at night, especially if you have to go out into an alley. Be cautious about these activities even during the daylight hours.

21. If you live alone, don't work in your yard or garage at night.

22. If you have a trusted friend you can check in with, make it a habit of doing so each time you come and go.

23. Don't hide an extra key outside. Rapists and burglars know all the best spots. Also, never leave your keys in your coat pocket when you check your coat or hang it in a public place. Similarly, don't leave your home key with a parking attendant. And never carry an identification tag on your key ring. If you lose your key and a rapist finds it, he'll know where you live and how to get into your home.

24. Keep your doors locked even if you're leaving for only a moment, such as to go to the neighbors', the pool or gameroom, the store, or just out into the backyard. Rapists and burglars are opportunists.

25. Don't leave underwear or bathing suits out on the clothesline, balcony or clothes rack at night. This could attract a rapist or "peeping Tom."

26. Don't leave ladders outside. They can easily be used by intruders to enter upstairs windows.

27. Be wary of male neighbors or casual male acquaintances who make it a habit of "dropping in" when no one else is home.

28. Even though it may seem like an obvious point, remember to keep drapes or blinds drawn when changing clothes, undressing or retiring for the night.

29. Have a plan of action so you'll know what to do in the event of an attempted assault. Your chances of preventing the attack are much greater if you're prepared beforehand. It's a good idea to role play and run through drills (not unlike fire drills) so you'll have a better idea of how to handle each situation you might encounter. Know the best escape routes from each room in your home. If you have an alarm system with a panic button, remember where the button is installed, and practice using it as part of your drills.

30. Keep a self-defense weapon handy at all times. But remember, guns are extremely dangerous to have in your home, especially if you have young children. Unless you are absolutely certain you could shoot an intruder, you are probably better off with a non-lethal defense weapon. A canister of powerful chemical defense spray is an excellent deterrent. The better chemical defense sprays can incapacitate an intruder for up to 30 minutes, allowing you time to run away and call the police.

PRECAUTIONS TO TAKE IN AND AROUND YOUR CAR

1. Always try to park in a well-lighted area. Never park in a remote area of a parking lot. Always park with your car facing out. Never park up against a wall. Also, try to avoid parking next to vans with sliding side doors. Muggers and rapists have been known to wait in such vans then jump out the side door to attack or abduct unwary victims.

2. Don't use stairwells in parking garages. Stairwells usually are too isolated to be safe. If necessary, walk up or down the ramp where you're out in the open and your screams could be heard.

3. Roll the windows up and lock your car every time you park it.

4. When you return to your car, have your keys in your hand ready to get inside the car as quickly as possible.

5. As you approach your parked car, be observant to make sure someone isn't hiding behind it or beneath it waiting for you to approach.

6. Never try to approach your car if something looks the least bit suspicious. Go back inside and call the police or security.

7. If a threatening person approaches you in a parking lot or garage, turn and go back inside. If you can't get back to safety, try to keep a parked car between you and the other person. If the person exhibits threatening action, scream for help. Sometimes, it's more effective to yell, "Help, dial 911, I'm being attacked." Also, try bumping a parked car on the chance that it has an alarm that will be activated by the bump.

8. Don't worry about being embarrassed over false alarms. If you feel threatened, do whatever is necessary to get other people's attention.

9. If you have to work late, have a friend or security guard accompany you to your car. If you take night classes at high school or college, try to leave when others are going to their cars, or have a security guard or faculty member escort you to your car.

10. Before getting in your car, be sure to check the floor of the back seat to make sure an attacker isn't hiding there.

11. Make it a point to lock all car doors as soon as you get in the car, every time, without exception, even if you're only going down the block.

12. If you think you're being followed, do not drive home. Drive to the closest fire station, police station or to the nearest well-lighted area where there are people around.

13. Know what to do if your car breaks down on the road. If it still is operable (as in the case of a flat tire), you may be better off trying to drive the car slowly to a safe, well-lighted place where you can get help. If you possibly can afford it, get a cellular phone for your car. Also, membership in an automobile club enables you to get roadside assistance if you have car trouble.

14. If you have car trouble on the road and help is unavailable, turn on your car's emergency flashers, raise the hood and tie a cloth on the aerial of your car. Wait inside the car with the doors locked and the windows up. If a motorist stops to help, crack your window slightly and ask him to call the police.

15. Carry a "Call Police" sign in your car and display it in your rear window if your car breaks down. Always wait inside your locked car until the police arrive.

16. If you want to help a disabled vehicle, don't get out of your car. Drive to the nearest well-lighted area where there's a phone and call the police.

17. If another car bumps your car from the rear in an apparent "fender bender," be extremely wary about getting out of your car to survey the damage. If you feel the least bit suspicious, drive to a safe place and then check the damage.

18. Don't pull over for flashing headlights behind you. If it is an emergency vehicle or the police, there will be flashing red or blue lights on top of the car. However, be suspicious of any unmarked car displaying red or blue emergency lights. Some rapists actually have portable flashing lights like the police use. Some even have authentic police uniforms and badges. If an unmarked car displaying these lights tries to pull you over, use your turn signals to acknowledge that you are aware of the car's presence behind you. Then, drive to a well-lighted area before pulling over. Stay in the car with your doors locked. If the officer asks to see your driver's license, pass it through your cracked window. If he tells you to get out of the car, ask that he call a supervisor. If he actually is a policeman, he will very likely understand your caution.

19. Always know the phone number of police or security personnel. You probably won't have time to look up a number in an emergency.

20. Be very careful around pay phones. Try to find a phone in a well-lighted, well-traveled area. Be watchful of everything and everyone around you while you are talking on the pay phone. If someone suspicious approaches you, immediately get back inside your car and lock the doors.

21. Don't pick up hitchhikers under any circumstances.

22. Always know the specific address of your destination and the safest route to take. Never take shortcuts through unfamiliar areas, and don't travel along dark, lightly traveled streets.

23. Let a friend or family member know where you're going, the route you're taking and the expected time of your arrival. That way, someone will know to come looking for you if you don't reach your destination within a reasonable time.

24. Always know the location of safe places along your route where you can go for help if you need it.

25. Try to do your shopping during the daylight hours. If you have to be out after dark, try to have another person with you.

26. Don't go to automatic teller machines at night, especially if they are poorly lighted or located in out-of-the-way places. Don't use any ATM, night or day, if suspicious-looking people are nearby. Be on the alert the entire time you are at the ATM.

27. Be leery of anyone approaching your car on foot while you are stopped at a bank or fast-food drive-in window. Keep your doors locked and your windows rolled up. Roll your window down only when it is your turn. If you feel threatened, drive away.

28. If someone approaches your car to ask for directions or assistance while you are stopped at a red light, do not roll down your window all the way. Crack it just enough to communicate. Drive off without responding if the person arouses your suspicion.

29. Don't drive strangers home from parties or clubs. You're playing a very dangerous game any time you allow a stranger inside your car for any reason.

30. If you arrive home after dark, leave your headlights on until you have the car in the garage and your house door unlocked. If your garage has a remote-control garage door opener, get in the habit of using it. That way, you can stay inside your locked car until you have closed and locked the garage door behind you.

31. Keep a self-defense weapon in your car and

know how to use it. Remember, however, that it is against the law in most states to carry a handgun in your car. Besides that, guns are very dangerous unless you know how to use them--and unless you are sure you could use them against an assailant. A good alternative is a canister of powerful chemical defense spray that will incapacitate an attacker for up to 30 minutes. Purse size canisters are available that clip onto a key ring. The key ring should have a key release so you can carry your protection in one hand and your keys in the other. Some chemical defense sprays have a range of six to ten feet, which enables you to keep an attacker from getting too close. It's legal to carry such sprays in most states.

PRECAUTIONS TO TAKE ON THE STREET

1. Stay alert and walk with a purpose. The rapist is looking for a woman who appears vulnerable--a woman who apparently is not paying attention to her surroundings, looks frightened or is unsure of herself.

2. If you are being harassed by someone in a vehicle while you are on foot, turn and run in the opposite direction. Try to head for lights and people. To continue the harassment, the driver will have to turn around the vehicle to follow you.

3. Be careful if someone stops you to ask for directions. If you reply, do so from a safe distance to prevent being grabbed and dragged into a car or an alley.

4. If you think you are being followed, don't go home. Instead, immediately head for the nearest area where there are lights and people. If you feel the least bit threatened, call the police.

5. Never hitchhike or accept a ride from a stranger. It is more than risky; it is extremely dangerous. Some rapists use their cars to get a woman alone. Once you're inside a car with a stranger, you've lost control of the situation.

6. When walking or jogging, wear clothing that gives you freedom of movement in case you end up having to run to safety.

7. Avoid being out alone at night. If you walk or jog in the evening, do it with several other people. If you live in a high crime area, avoid being on the street at night altogether.

8. Avoid walking on dimly lighted streets or through alleys and tunnels. Never take short-cuts through lightly traveled areas. Stay in well-lighted areas as much as possible.

9. Walk on the part of the sidewalk closest to the street, as far away as possible from shrubs, trees and doorways. You may even be safer walking in the street than on the sidewalk. Always walk on the left side of the street facing the oncoming traffic.

10. Stay away from public parks at night.

11. If a friend drops you off at home, have her wait until you are in the house before she drives away.

12. If you're in trouble, attract attention any way you can. Yell, "Help, dial 911, I'm being attacked."

13. Just because you're walking in your own neighborhood or an area that's familiar to you, don't drop your guard. Be alert and cautious at all times.

14. Use extreme caution when you're out jogging. Don't jog alone, especially along remote jogging trails. Try to jog in a group of people you know and trust. Be aware that some rapists dress up as joggers to blend in with other runners and arouse less suspicion.

15. If you have to walk between buildings on a school campus at night, try to walk in or near a group of other people. If necessary, get a campus security guard to accompany you.

16. Always try to expect the unexpected. As you walk or jog, try to develop an emergency plan of action in the event of an attack. And stay alert to everything going on around you. If you see something suspicious ahead of you, turn around and go in the opposite direction.

17. When walking to and from transit stops, walk confidently and directly. Stay alert to everything around you. Don't daydream. And never stop to talk to strangers. Plan the safest route to and from your transit stop, and use it. Make sure you know the location of safe places along the way. Always walk facing traffic, and keep a safe distance from vehicles parked on your side of the street. Stay away from shrubs, isolated areas, vacant lots, building doorways and alleys. Stay in lighted areas as much as possible.

18. When waiting for a bus, stay alert. Occasionally do a 180-degree turn to survey the area to either side and behind you. Do not lean against buildings or signs. Stand with your feet comfortably apart with the weight of your body evenly distributed so that you can react quicker if someone tries to attack you. Stand back away from the curb, and be wary of cars that pull up to the curb near you.

19. Avoid using bus stops in isolated areas if at all possible. Always try to wait at highly visible stops where there are other people around. You're most vulnerable when you're alone.

20. When you get on the bus, try to sit or stand as near as possible to the driver. Avoid sitting at the very rear of the bus. Try to sit in an aisle seat to give yourself easier access to escape routes in the event you feel threatened. Never let yourself fall asleep while you're on the bus. And don't stand near or in the midst of a group of men. If someone harasses you, tell the driver immediately.

21. When exiting the bus, be alert to others getting off at your stop. If you feel uncomfortable, quickly walk to where there are other people. If necessary, get back on the bus and go to another stop where you feel safer about exiting. Try to quickly survey the scene before you step off the bus. If there are suspicious people loitering nearby, it may be safer to stay on the bus and get off at another stop. However, make sure that you don't have to walk down isolated streets to get where you're going.

22. Carry a self-defense weapon with you every time you go out on the street. Here again, we suggest a powerful chemical defense spray. Most purse-size models of this spray come in a small leather case that can be clipped onto your belt or jogging pants. This is a good visual deterrent. It also can be carried easily in the palm of your hand, ready to help fend off an attacker in an instant.

PRECAUTIONS TO TAKE WHILE TRAVELING

1. Before you check into a hotel, inquire about security. If you are not satisfied that you will be completely safe, you may be better off finding another hotel.

2. Keep your door locked from inside the entire time you're in your room. Use every lock on the door.

3. Carry a portable travel lock for additional security on your hotel room door. Most are relatively inexpensive and are compact enough to easily pack in a suitcase. For extra measure, carry a portable intrusion/fire alarm as well.

4. If your hotel room has a peephole, use it before you open the door if someone knocks. If you don't recognize the person, don't open the door. Talk through the locked door. Do not crack the door, even if it has a chain lock on it.

5. If someone comes to your door claiming to be on the hotel staff, verify his status before you open the door. Most hotel personnel wear identification badges. Never open the door if you did not request a service at the hotel. Call the front desk and ask that someone be sent to check out the situation.

6. Be especially cautious in hotel corridors and elevator landings. Have your room key in your hand ready to open the door.

7. If you see anything that looks remotely suspicious, call the front desk or hotel security.

8. Use valet parking to avoid having to walk to and from the parking garage. If the hotel doesn't have valet parking, request that someone from the hotel staff accompany you to your car if you feel the least bit uncomfortable about walking alone. Don't be timid about it. You have a right to demand security at a hotel.

9. Rely on your instincts. If anything seems suspicious, report it at once to the front desk or hotel security. Don't worry about false alarms. Your safety is the most important thing.

10. When driving in a strange city, be careful not to venture into a high crime area. Before you set out for your destination, make inquiries at the front desk regarding the safest route.

PRECAUTIONS TO TAKE WITH DATES AND ACQUAINTANCES

1. When dating someone for the first time, try to do it in a group situation or by meeting him in a public place. This will give you an opportunity to assess your date's behavior in a relatively safe environment. If you don't feel comfortable with your date's behavior, the safest thing to do is terminate the date early in the evening.

2. Watch for signs that would indicate your date is a controlling or domineering person. (See Page 47.) If that's the case, he may end up trying to control your behavior. If he makes all the plans and decisions during the date, he might assume he has the right to make the decision regarding sex-- regardless of what you say.

3. It may be a good idea to go "Dutch" treat on casual dates. If the man drives and pays all the expenses, he might get the idea that he's justified in having sex with you--even against your will--because he is "just getting what he paid for." If you share the expenses, your date may be less inclined to expect sexual rewards later.

4. Be honest with your friend or acquaintance. When you mean "no," be sure that not only your voice but your body language (or non-verbal actions or postures) is saying "no." Remember, however, that nothing you do or say is justification for rape.

5. Make it clear early in the evening what you do and do not wish to do regarding intimate contact. When men receive such direct communication, they have a better idea of what to expect from the date and are less inclined to force a woman into unwanted sex. This is not meant to imply that anything you do would cause you to be raped. It is cited here only as an extra precaution.

6. If your date behaves in a sexually coercive manner--even after your direct communication about your intentions--you may have to use a strategy of escalating forcefulness. First, you should directly refuse by saying something like, "No, I don't want you to do that. Stop now!" If that doesn't work, you should escalate your protest in no uncertain terms with something like, "This is rape. I'm calling the police." Such a statement will cause most men to stop. If your date doesn't stop at that point, reinforce your refusal with whatever means you feel comfortable with, given the situation. Scream for help at the top of your lungs. If you are able to stop the attack, leave immediately if you can do so without placing yourself in greater danger.

7. Bear in mind that you are extremely vulnerable when you're under the influence of drugs or alcohol. Nearly 75% of the men and 55% of the women involved in acquaintance rape had been drinking or taking drugs before the attack. Only you can make the decision about the use of these substances. Using drugs and alcohol is risky behavior to begin with. The risk is greatly compounded when you do it in the company of men.

8. Be aware that it is very risky to accept a ride home or an invitation for a late night snack from someone you've just met. Furthermore, you're placing yourself in great danger if you invite the person into your home or apartment.

9. If you live in a college dormitory or apartment, be careful about who you invite to your room. Some men, particularly those who have little respect for women, might misinterpret your hospitality as an invitation for sex. Your decision on men guests in your room or apartment is a judgment call that only you can make. However, unless the person is someone you trust completely, it's not always prudent to have a male guest in your room. You should be equally cautious if the man invites you to his room. A 1988 survey of college students indicated that one male student out of 12 had committed acts that met the legal definition of rape or attempted rape.

10. It is a good idea to carry a self-defense weapon when you are dating someone you don't know very well. A small canister of chemical defense spray can be carried easily, clipped to your purse strap or your waist. Do not hesitate to use it if someone attempts to rape you--even if it is your date or an acquaintance.

DANGER SIGNS TO WATCH FOR IN A DATE OR ACQUAINTANCE

Rape counselors and rape victims alike recommend that you avoid a man who displays any of these characteristics:

* Verbally abuses you with insults or belittling comments

* Emotionally abuses you by ignoring your opinions or by getting angry and sulking when you initiate an action or idea

* Tells you how to dress, how to behave, who your friends should be or tries to control other elements of your life or relationship (On a date, he may insist on choosing the movie you'll see, the restaurant where you eat, etc.)

* Refuses to let you share the expenses of a date and gets mad or sulky when you offer to pay

* Feels possessive toward you and treats you like you're his personal property

* Gets jealous when you spend time with friends and other acquaintances

* Seems to be obsessed with you

* Talks negatively about women in general

* Drinks heavily or uses drugs

* Berates you for not wanting to drink, use drugs, have sex or accompany him to his room or apartment

* Is physically forceful with you or others (pushes, shoves, grabs, etc., to try to get his way)

* Has dramatic mood swings

* Acts in an intimidating way toward you (sits or stands too close to you, uses his body to block your way, speaks as though he knows you much better than he does, touches you when you tell him not to, etc.)

* Constantly makes sexual innuendoes about your actions or clothing

* Doesn't view you as an equal (possibly because he is older, more experienced or sees himself as being socially superior)

* Is unable to handle failure and emotional frustrations without becoming extremely angry

* Has a fascination with weapons

* Is cruel to animals, children or other people he can bully

PROTECT YOURSELF AT ALL TIMES

In an effort to protect themselves against sexual assault, many women have taken courses in Karate and other martial arts. These courses are fine if you ever have to do hand-to-hand combat with an assailant. Even then, however, it may be difficult or impossible to fend off an attacker who is stronger or armed with a weapon.

Some women carry knives or electric stun guns for protection. The problem with these weapons is that to use them you have to be within arm's length of your attacker. That's much too close for comfort.

Other women go so far as to carry a handgun in their car or purse. Some know how to use them, having spent time on the firing range learning how to fire and care for their guns. Many, however, do not.

Before you decide to carry a gun, there are several important things to consider. Unless you have a license to carry a gun, you may be breaking the law. Also, in many situations, you might not have time to reach for your gun, aim and fire before you're attacked. Given the element of surprise used by many rapists, you virtually would have to walk around with the gun in your hand in order to repel an attacker. Finally, could you actually use the gun against your attacker? Unless you are absolutely sure you could shoot another human being, a gun is of little value. The assailant might take your gun and use it against you or someone else. And what if you fired and missed your assailant and the bullet struck an innocent person? We urge you to think long and hard before you decide to carry a handgun.

As stated earlier, one of your best self-defense weapons is a canister of powerful chemical defense spray with a mixture of CS tear gas and capsicum. Since it is a non-lethal chemical, the spray empowers you with a weapon that doesn't require a life or death decision. Also, many such chemical defense sprays are effective from as far as six feet away, allowing you to keep a potential attacker from getting close enough to grab you. Equally important, you can carry a canister of chemical defense spray at the ready in the palm of your hand.

If you feel threatened by someone approaching you, aim the spray at the person's face and issue a firm warning like, "Stop right there" or "Back off!" In some cases, the mere act of commanding the assailant to stop and aiming the spray at his face may deter him. If the assailant doesn't halt at your command, fire the spray at his face. The chemical should immediately immobilize your attacker.

Leave the area at once. Go to a safe place and call the police to report the incident.

A WORD OF CAUTION: If you decide to carry a chemical defense spray, make sure it is a reliable, high-quality product. There are various types of chemical defense sprays available for personal protection, and some are better than others. One of the most effective is a mixture of CS tear gas and capsicum, often used as a riot control agent by the police and military. It can produce a severe burning sensation to the eyes and skin, involuntary eye closure, coughing, a chocking feeling and dizziness. The effects can last up to 30 minutes, giving you time to leave the scene and call the police. Before you decide to carry a chemical defense spray, check the laws in your area. Although you can legally carry chemical defense sprays without restriction in most states, several states and municipalities require you to have a license.

Don't let any self-defense weapon lull you into a false sense of security. Your best defense is to stay out of threatening situations. Common sense is the best weapon of all!

INDIVIDUAL REACTIONS TO SEXUAL ASSAULT

Do you know what you would do if you were actually confronted with the threat of sexual assault? Everyone reacts differently to a crisis, particularly one on the scale of a sexual assault. Your individual reaction likely will be influenced by such factors as your family life, your religious convictions, how you interact socially with others, your physical condition and your basic personality traits. The circumstances of the attack and your perception of the assailant also will influence your reaction.

Since you can't know in advance either the circumstances or who your assailant might be, it is important to think ahead to the different situations you might encounter and what your individual reaction might be. Ask yourself these questions:

1. Would it be more important to come away with the least possible physical injury, even if it meant being forced to submit to the attacker?

2. Would you fear the actual rape more than you would fear physical injury?

3. Would the thought of being sexually assaulted make you so mad that you'd rather face the risk of physical injury than be forced to submit?

4. Would the safety of other family members be more important than either rape or injury?

5. Would you be physically able to resist an attack?

Having answers to these questions in advance will help you decide the tactics to use in the event of an attempted rape. You will probably have to make split-second decisions at the time of the attack, so it's best to do a little self-analysis in advance to determine what your reaction would be.

TACTICS TO USE IF ATTACKED

Hopefully, you will never be in a situation where you have to decide on a tactic to ward off a rapist. In a real sense, it is a guessing game that takes place under extreme duress and involves making instant decisions that can have life or death consequences.

The tactics outlined below generally involve situations where a rapist has a victim in his clutches. Even after taking all preventive and precautionary measures discussed earlier, you still might find yourself in the grasp of a rapist, either someone you know or a total stranger. It's almost impossible to spot a rapist in advance since many of them give the appearance of being ordinary people. And most of them are masters of surprise and ambush. Therefore, it's important to consider the different tactics to use in case you find yourself in a situation where an attack is imminent.

Unfortunately, there are no blanket procedures that will successfully repel a sexual assault. What may have worked for one woman may not work for you. However, by knowing some of the tactics that have helped other women escape from their assailants, you'll at least have the basis for formulating a plan.

In a rape attempt, fear and panic are almost certain to be the first reactions. But if you are to repel the attack, keeping a clear head is of paramount importance. Also, the time, place and other circumstances of the attack will have a bearing on your reaction. There are no clear-cut rules. Each situation, assailant and victim is unique.

1. Scream for help or make noise.

Screaming for help is usually more effective when you have some advance warning of an attack; it is only useful if there are people near enough to hear the noise and come to your aid.

Sometimes screaming, "Call the police, I'm being attacked," (instead of "Rape" or "Help") gets more attention than a blood curdling scream. If you can get close enough to a window (either inside or outside), break it and yell the same thing. If you want people to help you, you need to scream specific instructions to get the appropriate help.

Before you choose to scream or make noise, you must weigh the odds of it working. Your screams might antagonize your attacker. He might become angrier, causing him to beat or strangle you to keep you quiet.

2. Run away if you can.

Under the right circumstances, this might be your best bet. It also could be risky, depending on whether your attacker can and will run fast enough to overtake you. Unless you are reasonably certain you can get a good lead and reach safety before he can catch you, this will be a difficult choice to make. Your attempt to flee may be part of the rapist's fantasy, and it may cause him to violently vent his anger on you should he catch up with you.

If you decide to run, make sure you have some place to go, such as through a doorway you can lock or barricade behind you, to your car or to a place where there are people who can help you.

Remember, fear and panic will probably be your first response to the assault. But your chances of eluding your attacker will be much greater if you can control your emotions. A clear head will allow you to act quicker and more decisively in the event your attacker drops his guard.

3. Use unusual behavior.

An attempted sexual assault is a crisis situation in which the normal rules of behavior do not apply. Nothing you do is inappropriate during a rape attempt.

Acting crazy, making yourself vomit, releasing your bowels or bladder--all these have been used with some degree of success during rape attempts. Your own ingenuity is your best guide.

Doing something the assailant doesn't expect may terminate or delay the attack since your attacker may be the type of man who needs to be in control. He may find it difficult to cope with something he hadn't anticipated.

Remember, however, that every rape and rapist is different. No matter what you try, you may be running the risk of physical injury, particularly if your behavior further antagonizes your attacker.

4. Try to gain a psychological advantage.

During the first few moments of an attack, you may be too terrified to utter a sound. That's perfectly normal. But if you have prepared yourself in advance for the possibility of sexual assault, the shock will not be as great. You might be able to gain a psychological advantage by talking to the rapist.

The key to this tactic is to speak calmly and sincerely as one human being to another. However, try not to beg, plead, cower or make small talk. Many times this is what your assailant expects you to do, and it may be just what he wants to hear as part of his rape fantasy.

You might try talking to the assailant about something that interests you. It could range from your pet, a recent movie you've seen, a book you are reading, to a recent death in the family. The important thing is to attempt to give your attacker the feeling that you're seeing him as a person. Hopefully, that will make him perceive you as a person as well, not some object on which to vent his anger.

It also may help reduce his rage somewhat if you can say or do something that enhances his ego. Remember, though, you're trying to gain an advantage over your assailant. Don't preach or talk down to your attacker. It's possible that he thinks women are too "uppity," and knocking down a moralizing female might give him great satisfaction. He also may be thinking that if he can pull you down it will raise his self-esteem. It is very important to reach him in a way that will break through the fantasy he is acting out and allow him to see you as an individual with honest feelings and concerns, not an object. If something you are saying seems to heighten his anger, try to switch to another topic as quickly and smoothly as you can.

5. Fight back with all your might.

Before you decide to use physical force, keep in mind that rapists have the potential to inflict serious harm. All rapists are violent people, as indicated by the crimes they commit. If your assailant has a weapon, it's safe to assume that he's willing to use it.

Fighting probably should be used as a last resort, after everything else has failed. If you start out by fighting and lose, you'll have little or no opportunity to try another approach because your attacker most likely will be angrier and more suspicious of your actions.

In using this tactic you must be willing and able to inflict serious injury on your assailant. Surprise and speed of action should be used to your benefit. *Unless you completely incapacitate your attacker, you are likely to be in even greater danger.*

Your risks of receiving serious injury from your assailant are greatly increased when using such tactics as biting, scratching, pounding his chest with your fists or using a weapon that will not completely incapacitate him. Even victims with extensive training in martial arts are not always successful with quick chops or kicks to vital spots on the body. The struggle itself could even arouse or further enrage your assailant.

If you're going to fight your attacker, *use surprise and speed to your advantage.* For example, put your hands on the assailant's face and get your thumbs in the corner of his eyes. Suddenly, press in and back with your thumbs as hard as you can in an attempt to blind or put your assailant into shock. Another technique is to grab the assailant's testicles and squeeze or pull as hard as you can. This possibly could inflict immobilizing pain on the attacker.

Both of these tactics can be accomplished in such a way that the assailant is caught off guard by your attack. If used, however, they must be sure and quick, and you must be willing to follow through to insure the disabling injury of the assailant.

Once you choose to fight, try to control your breathing to give your body as much oxygen as possible without hyperventilating. Breathe in through your nose, and exhale through your mouth. Also, try to keep your weight evenly distributed over your legs and your knees slightly bent. Don't lunge or flail blindly. Keep your eyes open, and focus on the point of the body you are going to attack.

The ultimate goal is to survive the attack. Never forget that, *if a victim is forced to submit to a rapist, she has not consented.* She has merely chosen a survival technique. This has been validated in numerous rape cases across the nation.

In one case in Austin, Texas, the rapist was found guilty even though the victim asked the rapist to put on a condom before making sexual contact with her. Defense attorneys argued that such a request implied consent on the part of the victim. However, as prosecutors pointed out to the jury, the assailant had entered the victim's apartment uninvited and threatened her with a knife. The victim, fearing not only for her life but also fearful of the AIDS virus, asked that the attacker use a condom. Her request was purely for survival and personal safety and did not mean she was giving her consent.

WHAT TO DO IF YOU ARE SEXUALLY ASSAULTED

If you are sexually assaulted, your immediate concern will be in obtaining proper medical and psychological help. This help is available from a number of sources. Regardless of whether you plan to press charges, call the police immediately. The police will take you to a local hospital or rape treatment center. Police sensitivity to the trauma of the victim, as well as police procedures for investigating sexual assault, have improved greatly in recent years.

If you refuse to call the police, at least contact a physician or crisis counselor immediately. They can offer objective professional advice about the situation to help you decide how to proceed.

It is also important that others close to you--your husband, family members, fiance or boyfriend--get counseling as well. This will make them more sensitive to the trauma you are facing and give the insight needed to support you during recovery.

Carefully consider the following points:

1. Don't douche, shower, change your clothes or disturb the crime scene, even though it may be your first impulse.

2. Initially, prosecuting your attacker may be the last thing on your mind. But after your immediate needs have been met, you may decide to assist the police, so be careful not to destroy any valuable physical evidence.

3. Some victims feel strongly about wanting to see the offender caught so that he will not be able to harm another person. Although many sexual assailants are repeat offenders, records indicate that rapists rarely retaliate against their victims.

4. If you decide to report the crime, the police will ask you some initial questions regarding the identity and location of the suspect, his direction of flight and whether he had a weapon. These questions may be asked en route to the hospital.

5. Procedures differ among hospitals. Generally, the victim will be asked her name, date of birth, brief medical history and perhaps some other general questions. You will first be checked and treated for any visible physical injuries. It should be pointed out that any treatment you receive will be strictly at your option.

6. A rape examination includes a complete internal examination performed by a qualified physician. This is done to establish the extent of any injuries as well as to collect specimen which can be used as evidence should you decide to press charges against your attacker. When appropriate, you will be offered medication to prevent venereal disease or pregnancy. However, any decisions about medication or other medical procedures are strictly up to you.

7. Usually, if your physical and mental condition permit, you will be asked to give a formal statement as soon as possible after the medical examination. The investigating officer will ask only questions that are relevant to the investigation. The police will ask you for a complete description of the assailant and where the actual assault took place. The police also will want to know how long the suspect was present, what he may have left behind or touched (such as a light switch, bed post, chair, etc.) and other relevant information. You will be asked to give the details of the assault which will more than likely elicit very painful emotions. However, these questions are necessary to establish all the facts of the case and will only be asked when you feel you are ready to handle them. In some jurisdictions, the police will want to take photographs to document your injuries as trial evidence.

8. Should you decide to press charges against your attacker, the state will handle the case. Prosecuting attorneys will proceed if they believe they have enough evidence for a case. Prosecution can be a long and complicated process.

9. Remember that you are not on trial; the defendant is. But under the criminal justice system the accused party is presumed to be innocent until proven guilty.

10. The prosecuting attorney will inform you of what to expect in the trial and may go over certain questions again. The probability of conviction may vary depending on such things as the quality of evidence and your testimony. Remember, many sex offenders repeat their crimes on others. Your decision to prosecute may save someone else from having to endure the pain you have suffered.

11. In many areas, help for victims with questions or doubts about prosecution is available from the District Attorney's Office, Victim Advocate Programs, Rape Crisis Centers, Rape Treatment Centers and various social service groups. The local police or the district attorney's office can give you the names and phone numbers of such organizations.

12. Above all, remember that *a victim is never to blame for a crime.* There is no more reason for you to feel guilt, shame or embarrassment than if you had been the victim of a mugging or other crime. You were an innocent party, and there are a great many people who are sensitive to your needs and eager to help you.

HOW FAMILY AND FRIENDS CAN HELP THE VICTIM OF A SEXUAL ASSAULT

The family and friends of a rape victim play an important role in the healing process. A woman who has been raped needs the love and reassurance, comfort and support of those closest to her. In a real sense, she needs the same kind of support you would give her if she had been seriously injured in an accident. Remember, she has gone through a painful, horrifying experience. In the aftermath, she very likely will face a major crisis in her life, and she will need your complete understanding and support to work through it.

Her most immediate need, of course, is for medical attention. It is important to discover and treat any physical damage or disease to prevent further medical problems. She also may wish to take measures to prevent pregnancy. Evidence must also be gathered in the event she decides to press charges against her assailant.

The decision to press charges should be left solely up to the victim. Possibly, she will see that it is the best way to direct her anger. It also may get a rapist off the streets and keep it from happening to someone else. However, she should not be pressured into the decision. In the course of a rape trial, the victim will have to tell her story to a roomful of strangers--and possibly defend herself against the accusations of defense attorneys. And in spite of all she does in court, there still is no guarantee that the rapist will be convicted. Even if she decides not to press charges, it is helpful if the victim gives police all the information she can. If nothing else, it may help the police track down the assailant and keep an eye on his activities. And should she change her mind about pressing charges later on, the police will have evidence to build their case.

During the period immediately following the assault, the victim may exhibit conflicting feelings and emotions ranging from anger and rage to fear and anxiety. She also may have feelings of guilt. She may express a hatred of men, have nightmares, lose her appetite, have trouble sleeping or feel depressed. However, these responses are perfectly normal. And with your understanding, care and support, they will pass with time.

As a friend or loved one, your pain may be great as well. Although you may want to put it out of your mind and forget it ever happened, you shouldn't try to make her forget. It's very important that she be able to talk it out with someone who understands.

Sometimes a rape victim is afraid to tell her family and friends for fear it will change their feelings toward her. The worst thing a victim can do is keep it bottled up inside her. Having a sympathetic person to talk to is crucial for her well-being. However, you should let her initiate any conversation about the rape. Don't try to force her to talk about it when she doesn't want to.

It is not unusual for both the victim and her family to feel a strong sense of guilt, thinking if only they had done something differently, the rape might not have occurred. Neither the family nor the victim have any reason to feel a shred of guilt for a rape. The only one who should feel guilt is the rapist. A victim is never to blame for the actions of a criminal, regardless of what the circumstances are.

Should someone insinuate that something in the victim's behavior made her somehow responsible, that person should be made aware of the truth about sexual assault: nobody wants to be raped, and nobody has ever said they enjoyed the experience. Rape is not sexual intercourse as we normally think of it. And it certainly isn't love making. Rape is a brutal, vicious assault, and rape victims do not willingly participate any more than do victims of robbery, battery or murder. Only someone who is extremely insensitive or completely ignorant of the facts would think otherwise.

Furthermore, should someone suggest that the victim somehow could have prevented the attack, that person should be made aware that rape victims are at great risk of serious injury or even death. The most important thing is that the victim survive the attack and come away with as little physical damage as possible. Remember, when a victim complies with a rapist's demands, she is not giving her consent. She merely is trying to survive.

Citizens Against Crime

"Saving Lives Through Education"

Defender Plus®
Quality Protection For Your Family's Safety!

A uniquely powerful chemical defense spray that combines CS tear gas, capsicum and ultraviolet dye, all in a solvent base.

Home Model (4 oz.)
with Safety
(Shoots to 12 feet)

Keep in all rooms where you might feel trapped, especially:
- by your bed
- by all doors
- by your shower
- in your car, boat and RV

Personal Model (½ oz.)
with Clip & Key Release
(Shoots to 6 feet)

The clip & key release make it easy to carry:
- in your hand
- attached to your keys
- on your belt
- on your purse strap

Additional Items Available:

Emergency "Call Police" Sign
Light Reflective

For All Cars:
- Gets safe help quickly
- Helps deter criminals
- Keep in your glove compartment

Door & Window Security Stickers
For Homes, Cars, Businesses

For All Doors & Windows:
- Creates illusion of security system
- Helps deter criminals
- Reusable, static cling plastic

Don't Be The Next Victim Book

An easy reference guide that discusses safety in five major areas:
- Protecting Yourself In The Home
- Precautions In & Around Your Car
- Precautions To Take While Traveling
- Precautions To Take In The Workplace
- Precautions To Take While Shopping

Turn the page for ordering information. (Note: prices may vary in your area. Use the toll-free customer service number for more information.)

For Fastest Service Call... 1-800-466-1010

NAME _____

ADDRESS _____

CITY _____ STATE _____ ZIP _____

(___) _____   (___) _____
DAY PHONE   HOME

(TAX INCLUDED)
QUANTITY   AMOUNT

FAMILY SAFETY PACKAGE .... $135.00 _____ _____
   4 Home Models   (Save $24.95)
   2 Personal Models
   2 Emergency Call Police Signs
   6 Door/Window Security Stickers
   1 *Don't Be The Next Victim* Book

PERSONAL SAFETY PACKAGE ...... $70.00 _____ _____
   2 Home Models   (Save $5.50)
   1 Personal Model
   1 Emergency Call Police Sign
   3 Door/Window Security Stickers

CALL POLICE SIGN PACKAGE ... $25.00 _____ _____
   6 Emergency Call Police Signs   (Save $5.00)

Personal Model w/Key Release .... $20.00 _____ _____

Home Model w/Safety Cap .... $24.00 _____ _____

Door/Window Security Stickers (6) .... $5.00 _____ _____

Emergency Call Police Sign .... $5.00 _____ _____

Personal Model Refill .... $11.00 _____ _____

Don't Be The Next Victim Book .... $6.00 (Save $2.95) _____

What Every Woman Needs To Know Book .... $5.00 (Save $2.95) _____

SHIPPING & HANDLING:
0 to $10 .... $1.35
$11 up to $35 .... $3.50
$36 up to $81 .... $4.00
$81 up to $134 ...... $5.00
$135 & up .... Add 5%

Order Subtotal = _____

Shipping & Handling = _____

TOTAL ENCLOSED = _____

☐ CHECK/MONEY ORDER   ☐ MASTERCARD   ☐ VISA   EXPIRES _____

CARD NUMBER _____ / _____ / _____ / _____

SIGNATURE _____

Citizens Against Crime

Citizens Against Crime, Inc.
P.O. Box 1241
Allen, TX 75002